FROM HEAD TO TOE

The Amazing Human Body and How It Works

by Barbara Seuling

illustrated by Edward Miller

Holiday House/New York

FOR ERIN MULLOY—B. S.
TO MY MOM AND DAD—E. M.

Printed in the United States of America

www.holidayhouse.com

First Edition

Library of Congress Cataloging-in-Publication Data
Barbara Seuling.
From head to toe: the amazing human body and how it works/by Barbara Seuling; illustrated by Edward Miller—1st edition
p. cm.
Summary: An introduction to the human body and how it functions, including simple experiments
which demonstrate the principles presented.
ISBN 0-8234-1699-2 (hardcover)
1. Human physiology—Juvenile literature. 2. Human anatomy—Juvenile literature.
3. Body, Human—Juvenile literature. [1. Human physiology. 2. Human anatomy.
3. Body, Human. 4. Body, Human—Experiments. 5. Experiments.] I. Miller, Edward, 1964– ill. II. Title
QP37.S489 2002
612—dc21   2001039693

For interactive activities
and reproducible sheets
to supplement
From Head to Toe,
go to www.edmiller.com

CONTENTS

THE AMAZING HUMAN BODY

THINK ABOUT THIS. The human body can grow, move, heal itself, bear weight, lift, twist, see, hear, feel, think, and reproduce itself. It adapts to its surroundings in order to survive. It has thumbs, which have enabled people to rise above the other animals by making it possible to do difficult tasks. The human body is a well-run machine.

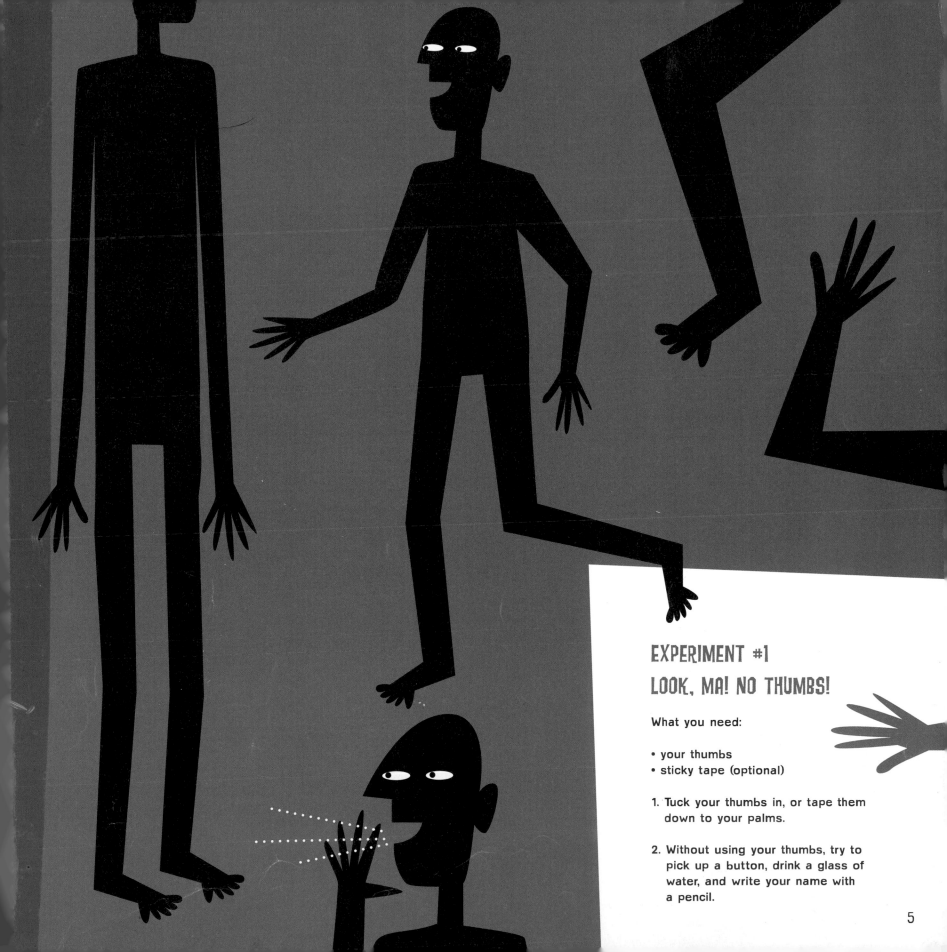

EXPERIMENT #1
LOOK, MA! NO THUMBS!

What you need:

- your thumbs
- sticky tape (optional)

1. Tuck your thumbs in, or tape them down to your palms.

2. Without using your thumbs, try to pick up a button, drink a glass of water, and write your name with a pencil.

Inside this amazing machine are systems and organs that keep your body working. You eat, and your stomach turns food into fuel, while the liver and kidneys help clean out waste. You breathe, and your lungs pull in oxygen, which your heart pumps into your bloodstream so it can reach all parts of your body to keep it running. You walk, and your brain sends messages to your muscles to tell them to move your legs. Everything in the body has a purpose.

Well, almost everything. Nobody knows why we have an appendix. It seems to be left over from ancient times when it was used in digesting food.

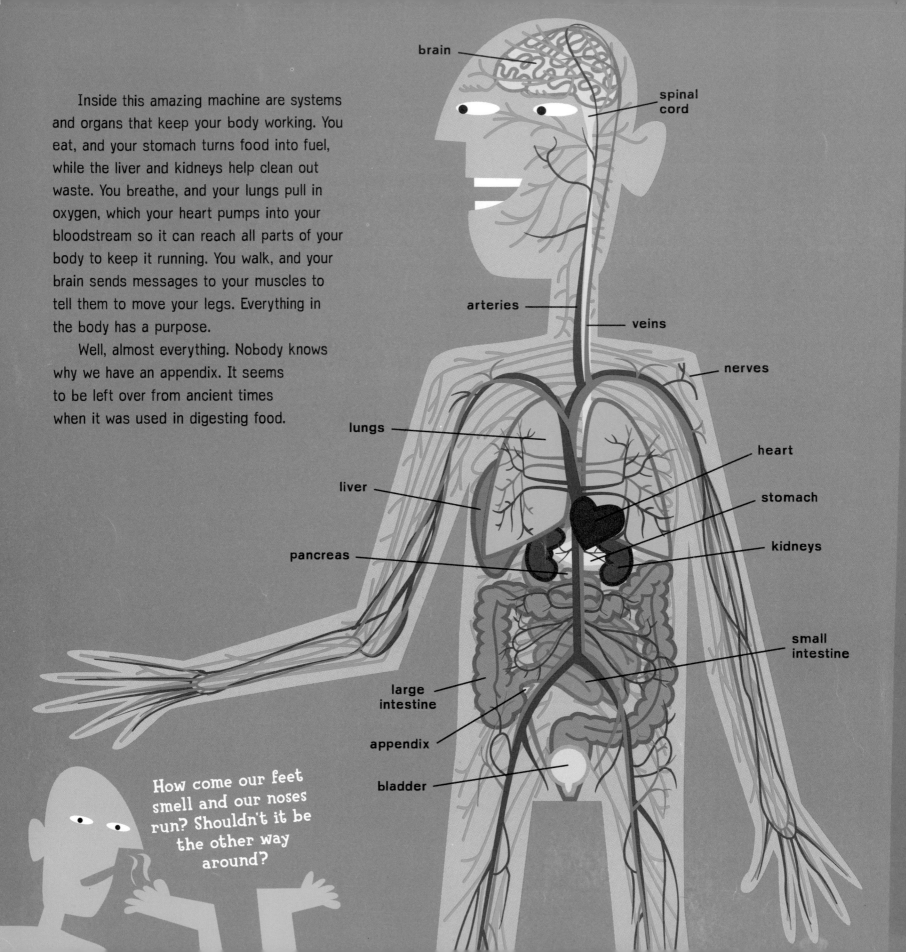

brain

spinal cord

arteries

veins

nerves

lungs

liver

heart

stomach

pancreas

kidneys

small intestine

large intestine

appendix

bladder

How come our feet smell and our noses run? Shouldn't it be the other way around?

You might think your belly button has no purpose, either. It doesn't anymore, but once it was your lifeline.

Before you were born, you floated inside a sac in your mother's belly. You got all the nourishment, food, and oxygen you needed through a lifeline called the umbilical cord. One end was attached to your mom and one to you, just where your belly button is now.

When it was your time to be born, out you came. The umbilical cord could no longer help you. It came off—it didn't hurt—and then you had to breathe air through your lungs and eat food through your mouth like everyone else. You became a person on your own. Your belly button is all that's left to remember how you were once attached to your mother.

We do know something about parts of the body we use. A good place to start is the foundation:

THE BONES.

umbilical cord

A SOUND FOUNDATION:
THE BONES

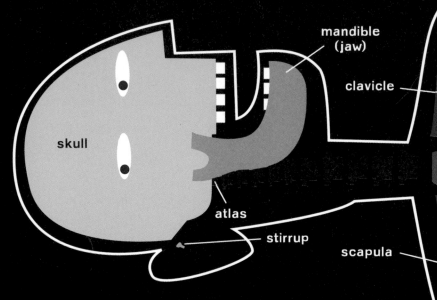

Bones make up your skeleton, the basic shape your body has before anything else is added. When you hear the word "skeleton," you probably think of the clickety-clackety bones of dead people rattling around in a scary movie. The fact is: every living person has a skeleton inside his or her skin.

humerus

mandible (jaw)

clavicle

vertebrae (spine)

skull

sternum

atlas

stirrup

scapula

ribs

WHEN YOU LOOK in the mirror, you see a shape covered in skin. What's underneath? You can feel certain hard places, like your knee, or your elbow, or your chin. You can feel soft places, like your cheek, or your stomach, or your thigh. What's going on under that skin of yours?

Well, be happy there is something under there. Without your bones, you would look like a Macy's Parade balloon before it's been blown up.

femur

stirrup

The biggest bone in the body is the femur, or thigh bone. The smallest is the stirrup in the ear.

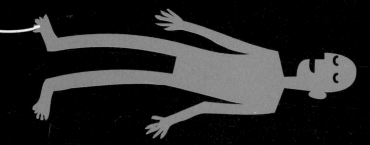

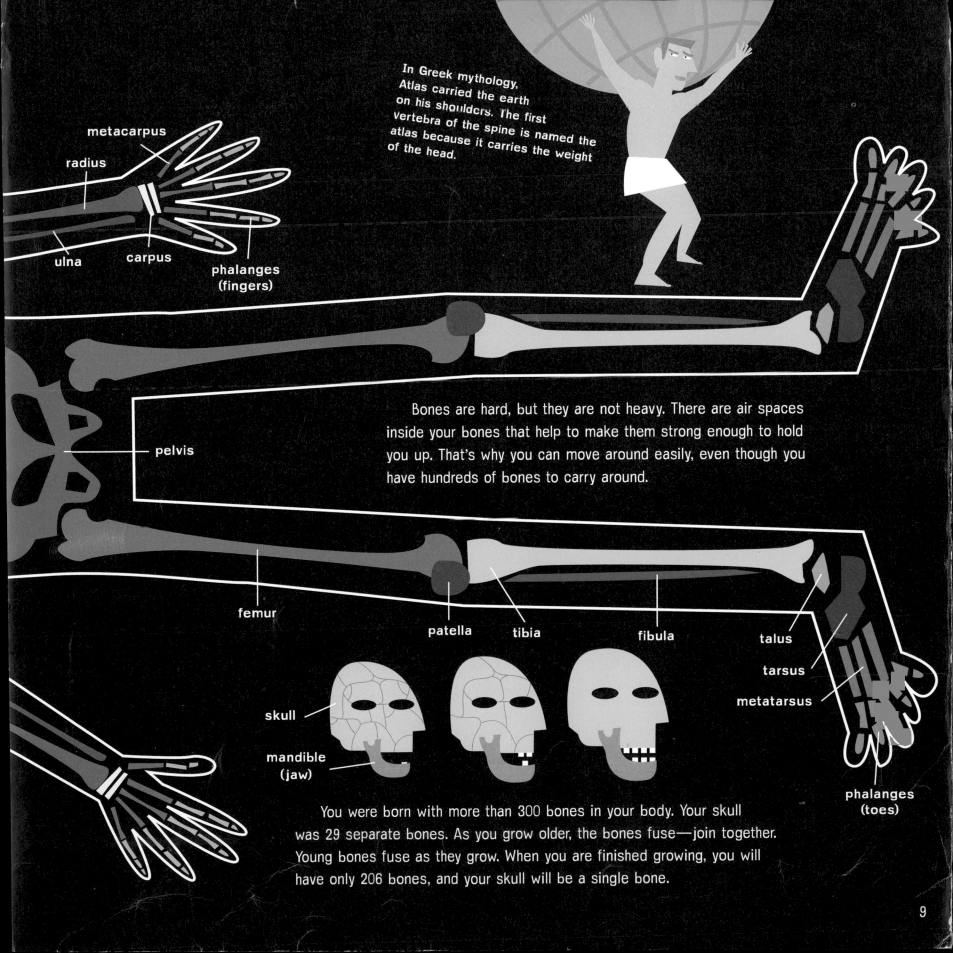

metacarpus

radius

ulna

carpus

phalanges
(fingers)

In Greek mythology, Atlas carried the earth on his shoulders. The first vertebra of the spine is named the atlas because it carries the weight of the head.

pelvis

Bones are hard, but they are not heavy. There are air spaces inside your bones that help to make them strong enough to hold you up. That's why you can move around easily, even though you have hundreds of bones to carry around.

femur

patella   tibia   fibula   talus

tarsus

metatarsus

skull

mandible
(jaw)

phalanges
(toes)

You were born with more than 300 bones in your body. Your skull was 29 separate bones. As you grow older, the bones fuse—join together. Young bones fuse as they grow. When you are finished growing, you will have only 206 bones, and your skull will be a single bone.

9

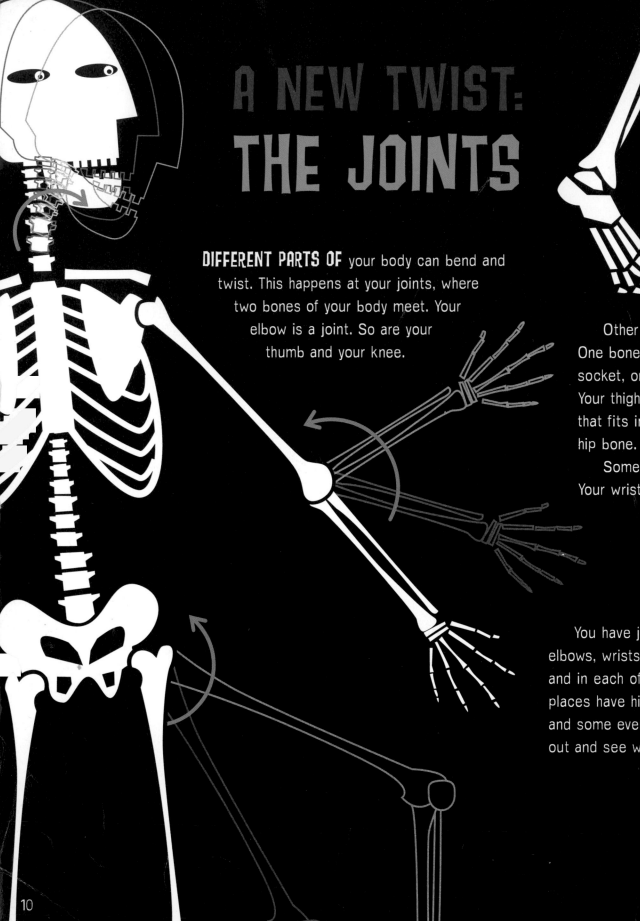

A NEW TWIST: THE JOINTS

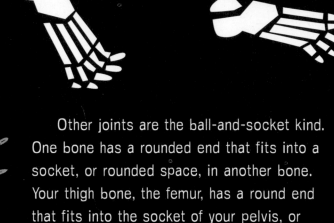

DIFFERENT PARTS OF your body can bend and twist. This happens at your joints, where two bones of your body meet. Your elbow is a joint. So are your thumb and your knee.

Other joints are the ball-and-socket kind. One bone has a rounded end that fits into a socket, or rounded space, in another bone. Your thigh bone, the femur, has a round end that fits into the socket of your pelvis, or hip bone.

Some joints twist around, or pivot. Your wrists and elbows are pivot joints.

You have joints at your neck, shoulders, elbows, wrists, spine, hips, knees, and ankles, and in each of your fingers and toes. Some places have hinge joints, some have pivot joints, and some even have two kinds at once. Try them out and see which kind they are.

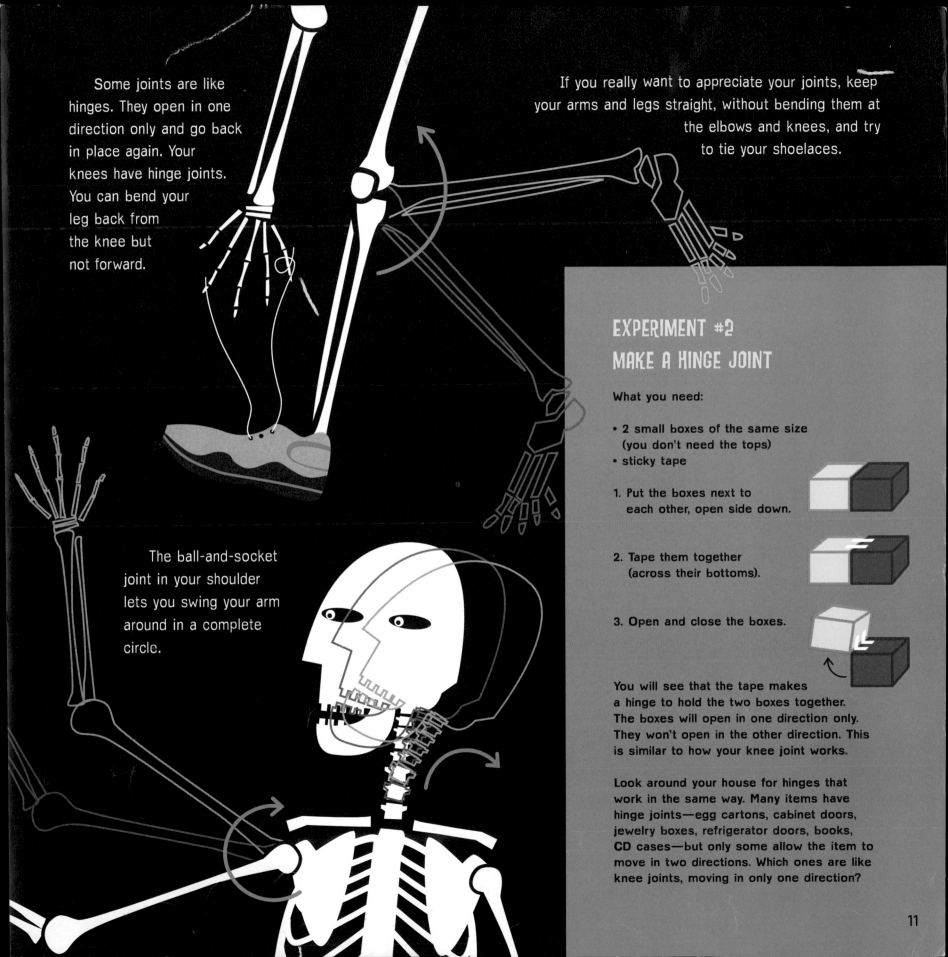

Some joints are like hinges. They open in one direction only and go back in place again. Your knees have hinge joints. You can bend your leg back from the knee but not forward.

If you really want to appreciate your joints, keep your arms and legs straight, without bending them at the elbows and knees, and try to tie your shoelaces.

The ball-and-socket joint in your shoulder lets you swing your arm around in a complete circle.

EXPERIMENT #2
MAKE A HINGE JOINT

What you need:

- 2 small boxes of the same size (you don't need the tops)
- sticky tape

1. Put the boxes next to each other, open side down.

2. Tape them together (across their bottoms).

3. Open and close the boxes.

You will see that the tape makes a hinge to hold the two boxes together. The boxes will open in one direction only. They won't open in the other direction. This is similar to how your knee joint works.

Look around your house for hinges that work in the same way. Many items have hinge joints—egg cartons, cabinet doors, jewelry boxes, refrigerator doors, books, CD cases—but only some allow the item to move in two directions. Which ones are like knee joints, moving in only one direction?

11

EXPERIMENT #3
MAKE A FLEXIBLE SPINE

What you need:

- a quarter
- a pencil
- 2 8½-by-11-inch sheets of thick paper
- scissors
- a hole puncher
- a long pipe cleaner or stiff wire
- 26 round beads approximately the size of a pea

1. Using your quarter as a guide, trace 25 circles onto your paper.

2. Cut out each circle with scissors.

3. Punch a hole in the center of each disk with the hole puncher.

4. Bend back a small bit of the pipe cleaner or wire at one end. String the beads on the wire, adding a paper disk after each bead.

5. When the wire is filled with beads and disks, bend back the other end of the wire so the beads won't fall off. Hold the wire upright. It will probably bend over.

This is how your spine moves when you bend. Your spine bones, or vertebrae, have many joints, so you can bend easily. The disks keep the bones from rubbing against each other and wearing down.

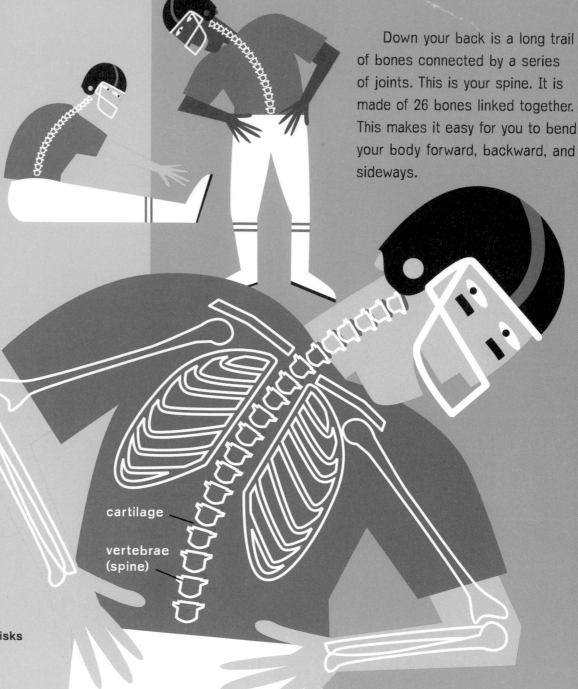

cartilage

vertebrae (spine)

Down your back is a long trail of bones connected by a series of joints. This is your spine. It is made of 26 bones linked together. This makes it easy for you to bend your body forward, backward, and sideways.

A tough substance called cartilage covers the ends of the bones where they meet. This keeps bones from grinding against each other. The 26 vertebrae that make up the spine don't rub against each other because there are disks of cartilage between the bones.

25¢

Your bones do more than help you to stay upright. Some of them protect your soft insides.

Your brain is covered by your skull, which works like a helmet, protecting it from bumps and bangs.

Wrapped around your lungs and heart is your rib cage, which is made of bones. Feel some of your ribs through your skin. You can find them on your side between your neck and your waist.

Even your spine protects an important part of your body. Under the hard bones of your spine is your spinal cord. This holds the nerves, like small wires, that bring feeling and movement to your body parts.

skull

brain

vertebra

spinal cord

lungs

rib cage

heart

Now you know what gives you your shape— your skeleton—but what makes it work? After all, you're a lot more than a bunch of bones.

13

MOVE IT!: THE MUSCLES

YOUR SKELETON IS the framework for your body, but it can't move on its own. The muscles attached to your skeleton make bones move. Joints between the bones allow your body to bend and twist.

Lift your arm. That took muscles. Your arm bones would just hang there if you didn't have muscles to pull them up and down. Now wiggle your little finger. Muscles made that work, too. More than 630 muscles move the various parts of your body, inside and out.

occipitofrontalis

temporalis

orbicularis oculi

zygomaticus major

HELLO!

It takes more than 30 muscles to smile. It takes 72 muscles just to speak one word.

sternocleidomastoid

trapezius

platysma

deltoid

pectoralis major

biceps

flexor digitorum profundus

serratus anterior

triceps

rectus abdominis

oblique abdominis

flexor carpi ulnaris

gluteus maximus

sartorius

rectus femoris

vastus lateralis

biceps femoris

Muscles are a little like strips of rubber that are stretched tightly between two points. Some are narrow, like rubber bands. Others are wider, like the skin of a deflated balloon. When you move your muscles, they move the bones to which they are attached.

gastrocnemius

tibialis anterior

achilles tendon

The great escape artist Houdini could escape locks, handcuffs, chains, even straitjackets by expanding and contracting his muscles.

EXPERIMENT #4
MAKE A MUSCLE

What you need:

- 3 paper towel tubes
- a ballpoint pen to make holes
- a large paper clip
- a bold felt-tip marker
- 2 long, slender balloons
- a piece of string about 3 feet long

1. Make holes through the tubes as shown, about 1 inch from the end.

2. Unbend the paper clip. Push it through the holes as shown. Bend back the ends so the tubes don't fall off.

3. Pull the middle "bone" up (this represents the upper arm). Label it humerus. Label the two side bones (representing the lower arm) ulna and radius.

4. Slightly inflate 2 long balloons so there is a bulge the size of a golf ball in the center of each. Tie knots in both ends of the balloons. Tip: Blow up the balloons several times to make them more flexible before you do this experiment.

5. Use a piece of string to tie one end of one balloon to the top of the humerus. Pull the balloon under the ulna and radius and tie it around both, close to the joint. (See diagram.)

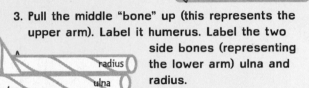

6. Tie one end of the other balloon to the top of the humerus and the other end two-thirds of the way down the ulna. (See diagram.)

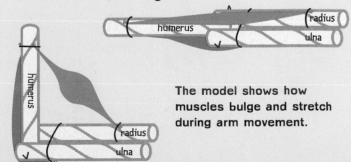

The model shows how muscles bulge and stretch during arm movement.

15

MAIN HEADQUARTERS: THE BRAIN AND THE NERVOUS SYSTEM

There are all kinds of cells, in all shapes and sizes, from skin cells and blood cells to brain cells and liver cells. The cells in the nervous system are called neurons.

Like a giant road map, the nervous system spreads out from your brain and spinal cord to every part of your body. The spinal cord is a thick column of nerves. Smaller nerves branch out from it. Neurons pick up signals—from a taste, a smell, or something you hear or touch—and, acting like messengers, deliver the signals to your brain. Then the brain sends messages back to the appropriate body parts.

brain

spinal cord

IF YOUR BODY had a main headquarters, it would be your brain. Your brain is the control center. But it wouldn't be much good if it wasn't connected to the rest of your body. The nervous system makes that connection.

Everything that is alive—grass, frogs, trees, people— is made up of cells. These cells, so tiny you need a microscope to see them, contain the material needed to grow, plus information that tells what each plant or animal is made of. Some forms of life are only one cell. Human beings are made up of trillions of cells.

neuron cell under a microscope

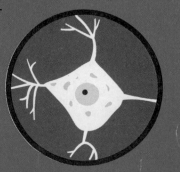

If the nervous system is like a map of thousands of roads and pathways, then the neurons are like billions of supersonic cars that travel those roads to reach your brain.

Imagine this. You come home from school starving. You sink your teeth into a chocolate brownie, but you don't taste anything. You might as well bite into an old sock.

YUCKY!

YUMMY!

When you put food in your mouth, neurons in your tongue send a message to your brain that you are eating a chocolate brownie, and your brain registers that you like it.

Most cells in the body die or are replaced, but the neurons you are born with stay with you throughout your whole life.

nerves

SALT

There are four basic tastes that are recognized by the human tongue: **SOUR, SALTY, SWEET,** and **BITTER.**

SUGAR

COCOA

EXPERIMENT #5
TEST YOUR TASTE BUDS

What you need:

- 5 small plastic cups with:
  1 teaspoon of sugar in one cup
  1 teaspoon of salt in the second cup
  1 teaspoon of unsweetened cocoa in the third cup
  1 teaspoon of lemon juice in the fourth cup
  plain water in the fifth cup
- 10 cotton swabs

1. Line up 4 cups, in any order. Have the water and 4 cotton swabs ready.

2. Wet the first cotton swab and dip it into the sugar. Touch your tongue with the swab. It will taste sweet.

3. Wet the second swab and dip it into the salt. Touch your tongue with it. It will taste salty.

4. Wet the third swab and dip it into the cocoa powder. Touch your tongue with it. It will taste bitter.

5. With the lemon juice, you don't have to dip the swab in water first. Dip it in the lemon juice and touch your tongue with it. It will taste sour.

6. Now close your eyes and mix up the swabs you just used. See if you can still tell the different tastes apart without looking.

Now try mixing two kinds of tastes together, like cocoa powder and sugar, or lemon juice and salt. (Use only a clean swab each time you dip, so you don't mix the flavors in the cups. To mix tastes on your tongue, use 2 or 3 different swabs and put them on your tongue at the same time.) Can you recognize two tastes at the same time? Three?

Would you say one taste is stronger than another?

More sensors are in your nose. Smells in the air from food, flowers, garbage, or anything with an odor enter your nose as you breathe. Neurons inside your nose send signals to your brain that the smells are pleasant or not. If someone near you passes gas, your nose tells your brain and your brain says,

"Move away!"

HOW TO
Eat with
a Fork

MEMORIES
of FIRST
GRADE

Besides being the control center for the nervous system, the brain is like your own personal computer, where your memories and knowledge are stored. Everything you ever learned, from tying your shoes and eating with a fork to riding a bicycle, is stored somewhere in your brain.

Many neurons are in your skin. When you touch something hot, for example, your brain receives messages that tell you it is hot and to pull your hand away.

HOT

If a fly lands on your nose, the neurons in your skin tell your brain there is something on your nose that tickles. Your brain sends a message to your arm and hand muscles so you can flick off the fly.

Part A:
Einstein's
Brain

Part B:
Einstein's
Brain

The brain of genius Albert Einstein was saved to be studied after he died. The brain got lost for a while but was finally found divided between a couple of Mason jars belonging to the scientist who had first saved the brain. The brain was then studied, but scientists still don't know for sure why Einstein's brain worked better than most people's.

Nobody knows exactly how the brain stores so much information. Scientists are still working on it. The most amazing thing about your brain is that you use it to think. Maybe someday you can use your brain to figure out the answers.

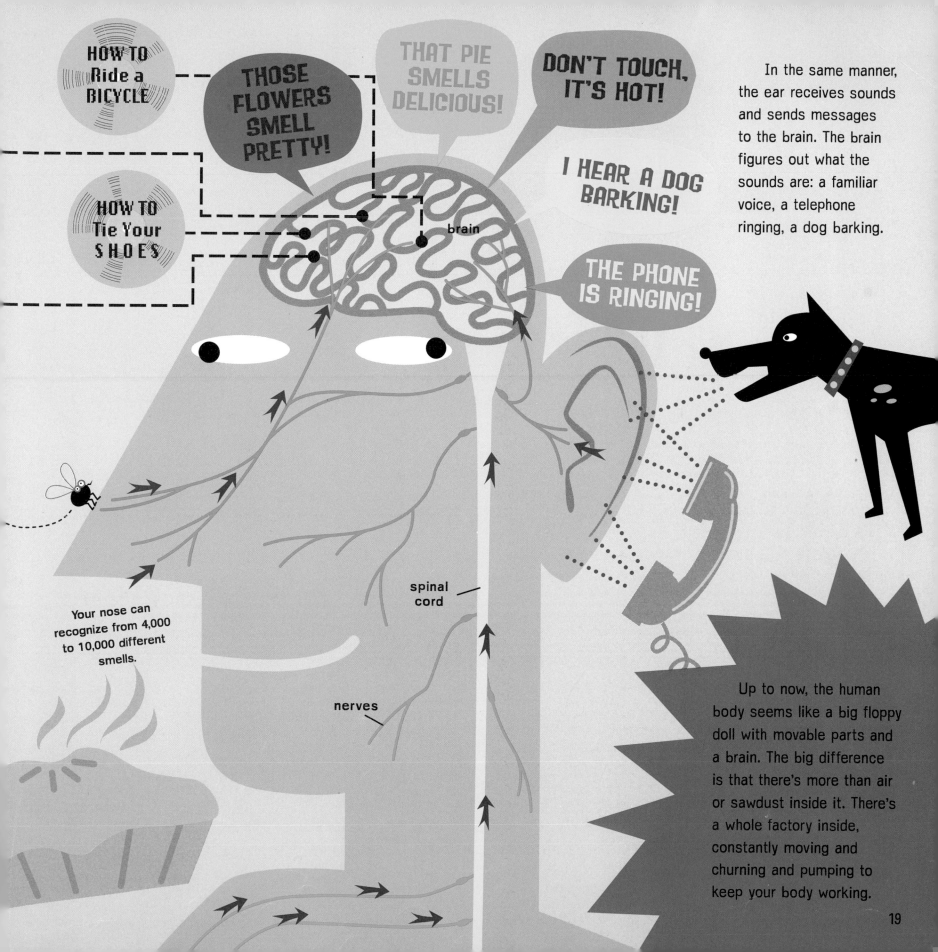

In the same manner, the ear receives sounds and sends messages to the brain. The brain figures out what the sounds are: a familiar voice, a telephone ringing, a dog barking.

Up to now, the human body seems like a big floppy doll with movable parts and a brain. The big difference is that there's more than air or sawdust inside it. There's a whole factory inside, constantly moving and churning and pumping to keep your body working.

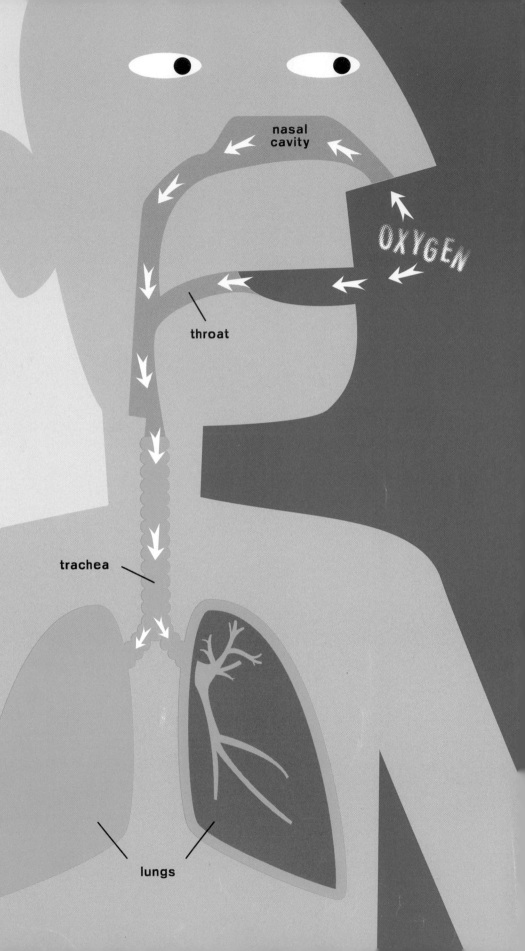

THE INSIDE STORY: THE ORGANS

THE INSIDE OF your body is like a factory where many parts and systems made of several parts work together to keep your amazing human machine going.

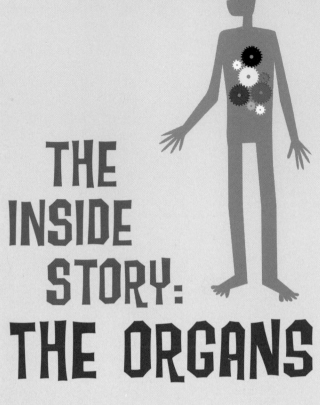

nasal cavity

OXYGEN

throat

trachea

lungs

LUNGS

You have two lungs, like stretchy air bags, that expand when you breathe in air. Your lungs use the oxygen that is in the air. When you breathe out, you get rid of the excess gases that your body can't use. Your lungs deflate like balloons after you've let out the air. You breathe in and out 15 to 20 times a minute. You don't have to think about it. Your body does it automatically.

You don't pull dirt into your lungs when you breathe because mucus in your nose acts like a screen to keep it out. When you sneeze or blow your nose, you get rid of the junk that collects there.

When you have a cold, it's hard to breathe through your nose because mucus has built up inside your breathing passages. Air has a harder time getting through.

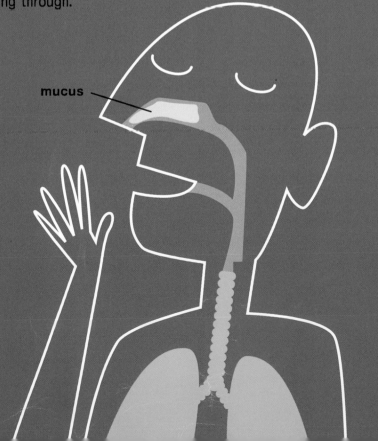

mucus

EXPERIMENT #6
HOW A LUNG WORKS

What you need:

- 1 liter-sized plastic soda bottle
- scissors
- a balloon
- plastic wrap or a piece of rubber film*
- a rubber band

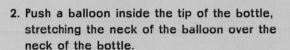

1. Cut the bottom off of a plastic soda bottle with the help of an adult.

2. Push a balloon inside the tip of the bottle, stretching the neck of the balloon over the neck of the bottle.

3. Cut a piece of plastic wrap big enough to cover the open end of the bottle with some left over. Place it over the open end of the bottle and hold it in place with a rubber band. Make sure the plastic wrap is as tight as you can make it.

*If you have trouble with this step, your plastic wrap may be too thin or too loose around the bottle. Get a piece of rubber film from a hardware store and use it instead of the plastic wrap.

4. Hold the bottle upright and pull lightly on the center of the plastic or rubber film. Air will make the balloon expand. Push the plastic film back in and the balloon will deflate.

This is how your lungs work. As you inhale, or breathe in, your lungs fill with air, and as you exhale, or breathe out, you let the air out again.

inhale   exhale

21

CARDIOVASCULAR SYSTEM

HEART

Your heart, a large muscle in your chest, pumps blood constantly. This blood flows through a network of arteries to reach all parts of your body.

Your heart is always pumping to keep your blood moving. Blood travels through the bloodstream that reaches every part of your body in a system of pathways called arteries and veins. Your heart never stops, even when you are asleep.

Put your hand on your chest. You can feel the valves of your heart opening and closing as it pumps your blood. This is what is known as your heartbeat. Your heart beats about 100,000 times a day.

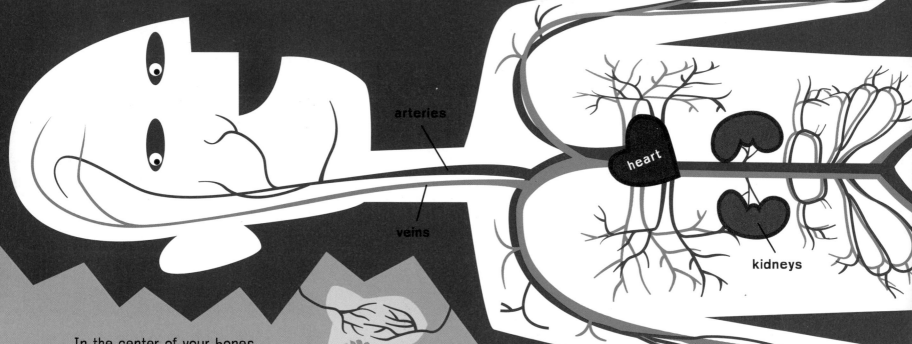

arteries

veins

heart

kidneys

In the center of your bones is bone marrow, a kind of factory where blood cells are made. Red blood cells carry oxygen through the bloodstream. White blood cells fight off germs. If you have a sore or blister, white blood cells make a gooey substance called pus that kills bacteria that try to enter the wound.

blood vessel

marrow cavity

bone

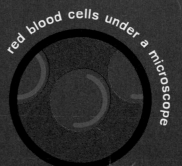

red blood cells under a microscope

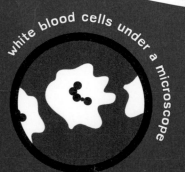

white blood cells under a microscope

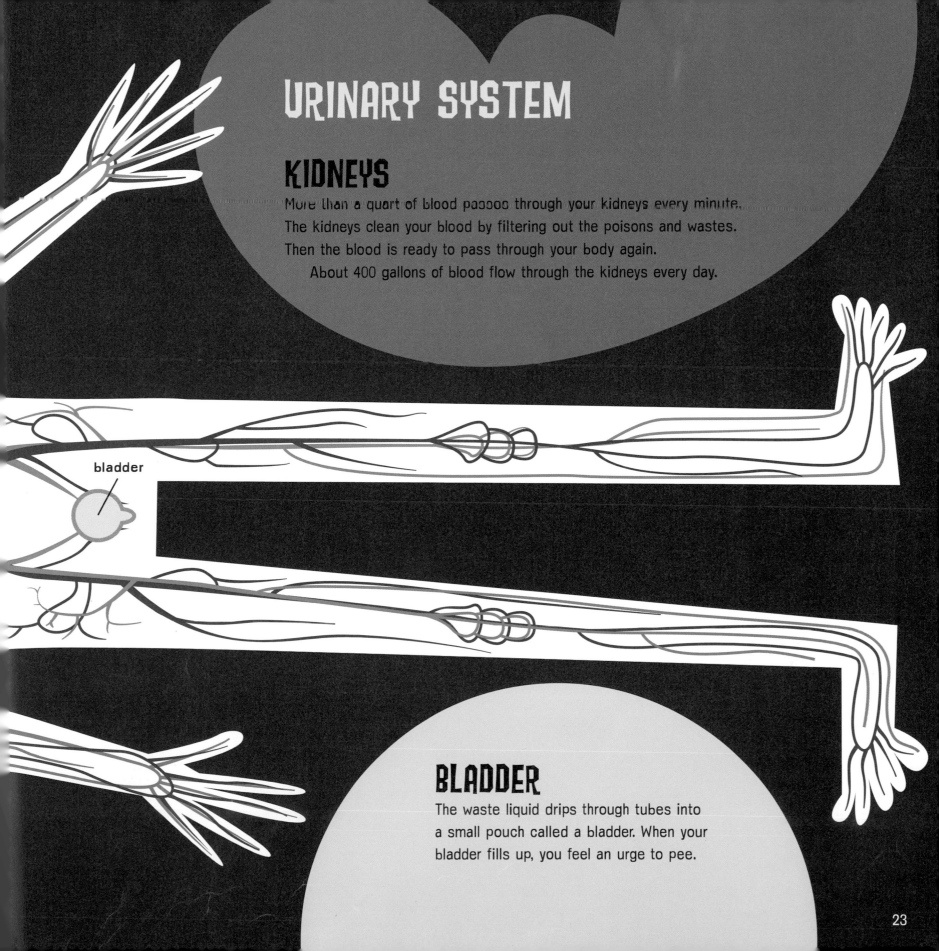

URINARY SYSTEM

KIDNEYS

More than a quart of blood passes through your kidneys every minute.
The kidneys clean your blood by filtering out the poisons and wastes.
Then the blood is ready to pass through your body again.
About 400 gallons of blood flow through the kidneys every day.

bladder

BLADDER

The waste liquid drips through tubes into
a small pouch called a bladder. When your
bladder fills up, you feel an urge to pee.

DIGESTIVE SYSTEM

Machines need fuel to run. Food is the body's fuel. No matter what kind of food you eat, it has to be chewed into small enough bits to go down into your stomach and be digested.

MOUTH

Spit, or saliva, helps you taste your food while you are breaking it down. It also helps keep your mouth and teeth clean and fight off bacteria that live in your mouth.

ESOPHAGUS

After your food is chewed, it goes down your throat through a long tube called the esophagus and ends up in your stomach.

STOMACH

Once the food enters your stomach, it is slowly digested. It mixes with acid that breaks it down into smaller and smaller pieces, until it is soft and mushy. The acid would burn a hole through the wall of your stomach if you didn't have a lining of gooey mucus in your stomach.

Bacteria help digest your food. They also create gas, which has to escape from your body. It comes out as burps or as farts. There is nothing unusual about these small gas explosions; almost everybody releases gas every day, even queens, kings, and presidents, no matter how famous or important they are.

OH, EXCUSE ME!

LIVER

Your liver is like a chemical factory. It filters out poisons from your blood and stores important substances like vitamins and minerals that you need for a healthy body. It also produces a chemical called bile to help to digest your food.

An adult human has about 26 feet of intestine. That's about the length of two average cars!

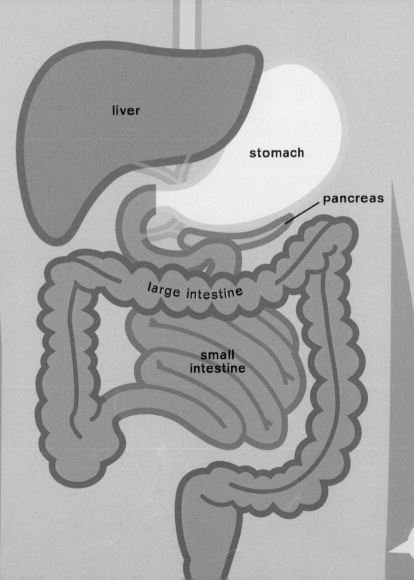

SMALL INTESTINE

The food passes into the small intestine, where it breaks down even more. Nutrients are drawn from the food and passed into the bloodstream. The bloodstream takes the nutrients on a journey to all the different parts of your body, giving some to each cell.

LARGE INTESTINE

Anything left in the small intestine that cannot be digested is sent to the large intestine. Water and minerals are squeezed out of it and the solid waste comes out of your body when you poop.

Food stays in your stomach about 3 to 4 hours before it leaves for the intestine. It takes another 3 hours to move through the intestine.

OUTER WRAPPINGS: THE SKIN, HAIR, AND NAILS

Your skin is made up of billions of tiny cells. When cells grow old, they die and fall off your body. Thousands fall off every minute. After you take a bath and dry yourself off, a fine powder rubs off your skin. It's made of dead skin cells.

The amazing thing is new cells grow from below to replace the dead ones. As a matter of fact, your entire body makes a whole new layer of skin every month.

IT'S A GOOD thing you have skin wrapped around you. It covers your bones and muscles, and keeps your insides from spilling out. It also keeps out water, dirt, and germs.

Your skin can get hurt, and then it can't protect you from everything. You can cut yourself on a sharp object or bruise your skin when you fall. If you touch something hot or stay in the sun too long, you can get burned.

When there is an opening like a cut in your skin, germs can enter your body and cause infection. That's why it's important to clean cuts. If a cut is small, it can be closed with a Band-Aid or a butterfly bandage. If a cut is big, the doctor may have to close it with stitches or special glue.

Under the top layer of skin is another layer, called the dermis. When you are out in the sun, Vitamin D is absorbed in this layer of your skin. However, if you get a bad sunburn, or any kind of burn, it can damage the cells in the dermis and leave you with a scar.

CROSS SECTION OF SKIN

Vitamin D from the sun's rays

hair

epidermis

hair follicle

sweat glands

veins

arteries

nerves

dermis

Skin color comes from a pigment in the dermis called melanin. Melanin protects the skin from the damaging rays of the sun. The more melanin you have, the darker your skin is and the longer you can stay in the sun without harm.

Although more melanin can be made in your skin cells by staying in the sun, a suntan is only temporary and will eventually go away. The skin color you were born with stays.

Your skin controls the temperature of your body. If your skin feels hot, you sweat. The sweat evaporates on your skin, cooling you down. If your skin feels cold, hairs on your skin stand on end, trapping air to make you warmer. This is how animals with fur keep warm in cold weather.

Once, people had a lot more hair on their bodies. Now when you get a chill or feel afraid, you get goose bumps, which are little bumps where hairs used to be.

27

The skin on your fingertips is more sensitive than on other areas on your hand. You can feel things and tell what they are more easily with the tips of your fingers than you can with the palm or the back of your hand. The ridges in your fingertips make it easier for you to hold on to things. These ridges also make your fingerprints.

EXPERIMENT #7
STUFF IT IN A SOCK!

What you need:

• an old sock (no holes, please!)
• several small, familiar objects that will fit in the sock

Here's a list of possibilities, but you can think of others: balloon, spoon, marble, coin, paper clip, safety pin, pinecone, rubber band, fork, Ping-Pong ball, watch, hair clip, marker, feather, piece of sandpaper, small rock, toothbrush, piece of string, crayon, button, magnifying glass, shoelace, chalk, pen cap, eraser, sponge.

1. Put about a dozen or more different objects into a thick, clean sock. These could be anything around the house. Try to find objects that have interesting textures or shapes.

2. Now take the sock to someone and ask him or her to try to tell what the objects are by feeling through the sock.

Notice how the person works with his or her fingertips to try to figure out each object. Fingertips are so sensitive that you use them to feel temperature, texture, shape, and sharpness more than any other part of your body.

Since no two people on earth have the same fingerprints, they can be used to identify you. Detectives identify criminals by matching their fingerprints to ones they have found at the scenes of crimes. Lost or kidnapped children are sometimes found and identified through fingerprints that are filed with a family's important papers.

EXPERIMENT #8
BE A FINGERPRINT DETECTIVE

What you need:

• 5 volunteers
• an ink pad, the kind you use for rubber stamps
• 10 unlined index cards
• soap and water for washing off the ink

1. Ask the first volunteer to write his name at the bottom of two different cards.

2. Ask him to put his right thumbprint over his name on one of the cards. Put this in Pile #1.

3. Take the other card and ask him to put his right thumbprint on the blank side. Put this in Pile #2.

4. Mix up the cards in Pile #1 (the ones with the name and the fingerprint showing) and lay them in a stack face down on the table.

5. Spread out the cards from Pile #2 in a row, fingerprint side up. Mix them around so you don't know the identity of any of them.

6. Take the top card from Pile #1. Lay it face up above the others.

7. Match it to one of the five thumbprints below. Look very carefully at the center of the print and any patterns you can find in the different lines. When you think you have identified the right thumbprint, turn over the marked card to see if you have made a correct match.

If you make a mistake at first, practice doing it again and again. You will get better at seeing patterns and matching up one print to the other. Then you will be a fingerprint detective.

Hairs grow out of tiny openings in the dermis called follicles. If your follicles are round, the hairs that grow out are straight. If your follicles are oval, shaped more like an egg, the hairs grow out curly.

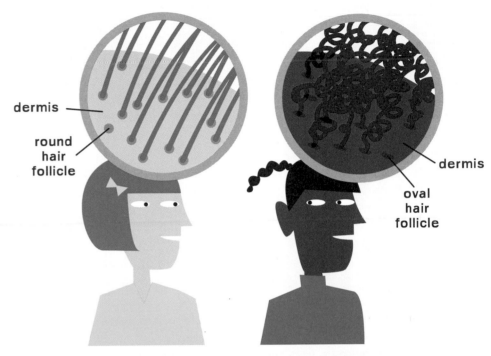

dermis

round hair follicle

dermis

oval hair follicle

Hair and fingernails are made of keratin, the same stuff that's found in animal claws, horns, hooves, and feathers. The hair and the nails that you see are made up of dead cells, so you can't feel it when they are cut. The parts of your hair and nails that are under the skin are living and growing.

keratin

Don't worry. Your nails won't grow into claws. That only happens in movies.

29

THE BODY SHOP

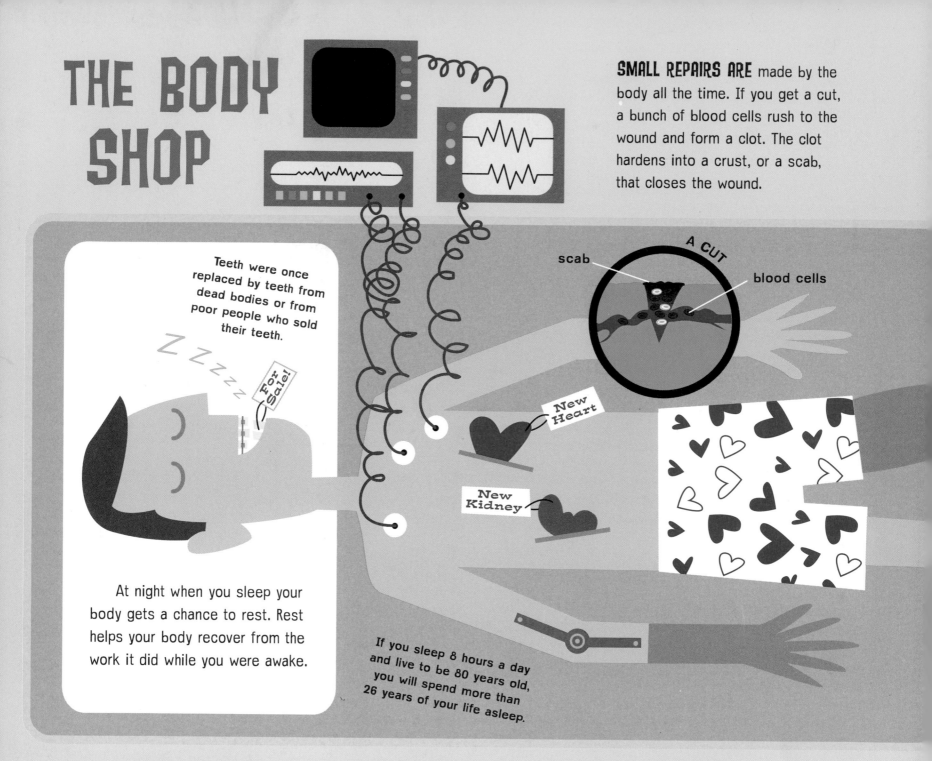

Teeth were once replaced by teeth from dead bodies or from poor people who sold their teeth.

For Sale!

SMALL REPAIRS ARE made by the body all the time. If you get a cut, a bunch of blood cells rush to the wound and form a clot. The clot hardens into a crust, or a scab, that closes the wound.

A CUT

scab

blood cells

New Heart

New Kidney

At night when you sleep your body gets a chance to rest. Rest helps your body recover from the work it did while you were awake.

If you sleep 8 hours a day and live to be 80 years old, you will spend more than 26 years of your life asleep.

Some repairs are too big for the body to do on its own. What happens when a body is injured, or damaged? Some people wear braces to help straighten weak or crooked bones or teeth. Others who cannot use their legs get around in wheelchairs.

Lifelike parts have been created to take the place of damaged ones. A crushed elbow can be replaced with a new elbow joint that moves just like a real one. An artificial arm or leg shaped like a real one can be attached to the stump of a limb so people can go on with their lives in a normal manner.

Pirates and soldiers engaged in battle often lost limbs that were later replaced with hooks for hands or carved wooden posts for legs. Remember Captain Hook, the pirate in *Peter Pan*? He had a hook to replace the hand that was snapped off by a crocodile.

YUMMY!

Sometimes surgery is necessary to make repairs. These days inside parts are also being replaced. Not only do people want to look better, but they want to live longer lives. Along with fingers and knees and hips, people are now replacing worn or damaged livers, hearts, and kidneys.

Scientists even grow new skin in laboratories. When a person's skin is too badly burned to heal itself, artificial skin may be used to repair the burned area.

Nearly 400 years ago, the Danish scientist Tyco Brahe lost the tip of his nose in a sword fight. He had it replaced with gold.

EXPERIMENT #9
MAKE A ROBOTIC HAND

What you need:

- 8½-by-11-inch piece of cardboard
- ruler
- pencil
- scissors
- sticky tape
- 4 rubber bands (flat wide ones work best)
- a plastic straw
- 4 pieces of string, 10 inches long each

1. Cut out a 4-inch square of cardboard for the palm.

2. Cut out 12 pieces of cardboard ¾ inches x 1 inch for the fingers.

3. To attach the finger strips to the palm and one another, line up the 12 cardboard pieces in 4 rows of 3 along one side of the palm. Leave a tiny bit of space between the pieces. Tape the finger joints to one another and the fingers to the palm.

4. Cut each rubber band so you have a long strip.

5. Tape a rubber band over the end of each fingertip. Then pull each band slightly and tape it to the palm.

6. Add another piece of tape over the rubber bands at the middle of each finger section.

7. Cut 12 pieces of a plastic straw, each ½ inch long.

8. Tape the straw pieces to the middle of each finger section and at the top of the palm.

9. Thread a 10-inch string through the straw pieces on each finger.

10. Tape the ends of the string over the fingertips.

By pulling on the other end of the string, you can make each finger bend at the joints. By pulling all strings at once, you can make a "fist."

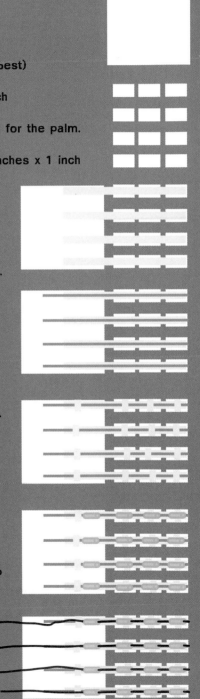

31

So far, no one has replaced a whole brain—but scientists have been successful in replacing certain cells in the brain. Nobody knows what may happen in the future. There probably won't be any part of the body that cannot be replaced some day.

Imagine an ad in the year 2050.

What would you do? Exchange your brain for a smarter one or your muscles for bigger, stronger ones? Would you ask for a better voice so you can be lead singer in a band?

Only time will tell how far we will go in keeping our bodies up and running.